Body La

Discover and Understand the Psychological Secrets Behind Reading and Benefitting From Body Language

Harvey Segler

TABLE OF CONTENTS

Introduction

I want to thank you and congratulate you for purchasing the book, *Body Language.*

This book contains proven steps and strategies on how to effectively read body language, and gain the great benefits that come from reading it. We as people are always communicating. We do it with our words and with our bodies.

There are times when our words say one thing, and our bodies say another, however. Perhaps you have done this yourself. You say you are fine with something for any number of reasons, but in truth you aren't fine with it. Outside your words say you are, but if someone were to watch your body language, they would know that you aren't.

And that's just one example. If you want to truly become a master of social interaction, you have to learn how to read body language, and how to respond to that reading effectively.

.

This book is going to show you how to read another person's body language effectively so you can respond to it in the way they need, and change the situation for a better outcome.

Thanks again for purchasing this book, I hope you enjoy it!

Chapter 1 – Another Real Language

You may remember having the option to learn a new language when you were in high school. For some of you, it was a requirement. You had to take a year or two of another language, hands down, no choice, no questions asked.

You were, however, given the opportunity to choose the language you wanted to learn, whether it be French, German, Spanish, or even American Sign Language were options for some schools. For all of you that opted for the sign language, I'm sure you remember that there were the kids that argued that signing with your hands wasn't a "real" language, and therefore it wasn't a "real" grade.

If you had taken that course, however, or if you have ever had the opportunity to witness two people conversing in sign language, you know for a fact that it is indeed a real language and it's difficult to learn at first.

Then we have those dead languages. The ones that nobody speaks anymore, or the ones that so few people speak that the language is no longer classified as living. You're probably thinking of Latin right now. Even though there are countless medical, legal, and even religious terms that are Latin, this language is still considered to be dead.

There is yet another language that is alive and well. Perhaps the most universal of all languages, as anyone can read it without either person saying a single word.

I am referring to body language.

But, you argue, that's not a real language.

Let me stop you there for a second. Body language, better known as *nonverbal communication* in social science, is the display of an emotion or thought without ever saying a word.

Still not convinced?

Consider this: we as people are fascinated with body language. If we see two people across the street making wild gestures at each other we automatically pause to see what's going to happen next. If we see through the window two people being close and passionate, we can assume they are going to take it further.

If a celebrity or high ranking official makes a gesture or refuses a gesture, we talk about it for weeks on end.

Why?

Because we want to know the drama that is going on behind it. We want to know why the person made the gesture or didn't. We want to know why the people are arguing or if they are going to take it further. We want to know more about the story, because the part of the story we read from their body language wasn't enough to satisfy our curiosity.

While you can spend your entire day chasing after the latest gossip based on body language, you can also see it taking place all around you in your day.

Your date says they don't care where you go for dinner, but you can "just tell" the entire evening that they didn't want to go to the restaurant you chose. Your boss says good morning to you as always, but you wonder if something is wrong because of the way the interaction took place.

You don't feel the person at the customer service counter treated you with respect, even though they didn't say anything impolite.

And, we have all been in that situation where we can use the phrase, "He/she didn't say anything, but they didn't have to. I could just tell..."

In all of these situations, you were reading body language.

Remember everyone else is reading body language throughout the day the same way you are. That means they are reading you.

What does your body language tell the world?

Exercise 1.

I want you to take a moment right now, and analyze how you are sitting. Whether you are in an office, in the library, at home, or wherever, don't change a thing about yourself.

Think about how you are sitting. Are you crouched over? Are crossing your legs? Are you folding your arms?

Are you taking up as little space as possible? Or, on the other hand, are you taking up as much space as possible?

How are you presenting yourself to those around you right at this moment?

Have you analyzed yourself? Ok, good.

What you just analyzed about yourself is called a nonverbal expression

We all subconsciously express ourselves this way, whether we give it any thought or not. The way you sit, stand, relax, or speak to people will spring from your perception of yourself.

What, what?

That's right. We all carry ourselves according to the power and dominance we feel we possess. And this isn't just true of humans, animals do it, too.

If you have ever seen a porcupine or a badger, you know that they make themselves as large as they can when they are confronted by danger. They do this because they are showing off to whatever it is in front of them.

Bears do it, birds to it. Primates do it. All across the board you see different animals that do this same thing.

Imagine a turkey or a peacock. They strut around with their tails spread behind them, open wide for the world to see. You can tell just by looking at them they don't fear anything. They are presenting themselves to the world as they see themselves... the best.

People do the same exact thing. If you stop and think for a moment, consider the confident people you know. They don't slump, they don't stare at the floor when they speak with someone. They don't "mouse" around. They stand tall, hold their head up high, and take the world in.

Consider the athletes you see in the Olympics or on sports games. Whenever one of the athletes does well, what does he do?

He extends his hands up and out in a V shape, looking slightly up to the sky, opening his body wide. We have all seen it, and many of us have likely also done it when we have won something we were working hard for. This is an expression of power and dominance.

It is interesting to note, this is an act that is born into us. In other words, we don't learn to take on that form when we win based on what we see in the world around us. A person that is blind from birth will do the same exact thing if they have this feeling, even though they have never seen it done by anyone else before.

But what do we do when we feel powerless?

The exact opposite. When we feel like we lost, or that we can't win at anything (literally or figuratively) we do the opposite action. We pull our arms in. We draw our legs in.

We take up as little space as we possibly can, trying not to make contact with the world around us. Think about the people you have seen that do this. Think about your reaction to them. If they are someone you don't know, you probably wonder what is wrong with them.

If you do know them, you wonder if there is something bad that happened, or if you know what happened, you know why they are doing that, and you may describe it as 'pouting' or 'sulking'. Whatever your thoughts are behind it, you read what the person is feeling based on what they are doing in either sense.

We call it such things as 'pride', 'arrogance', 'confidence', 'insecurity', and so on, but these judgements are all based on what we perceive by the person's body language. You never have to say a single word to the person, you don't have to know what happened to them or what they accomplished, all you have to know is how they are holding themselves or presenting themselves.

The world is thinking the same thing about you based on how you present yourself.

This truth suddenly makes it all so much more personal. Take a look around the room you are in, then take another look at yourself. Do you see people that appear to be closed off? Do you see people that are taking up a lot of room, even if they are just sitting in a single spot?

Now look at what you are doing. Are you open wide? Looking people in the eye as they walk by, or are you closed down?

Whichever the answer is, I want you to ask yourself if how you are sitting is a reflection of yourself. Do you feel closed off and powerless? Do you feel powerful and dominant?

Chances are, you are sitting just how you feel on the inside, or if you aren't, you are sitting in a way that is telling the world that you aren't powerful, even if you feel that you are.

You spend your day analyzing what other people are thinking and feeling, all based on what you see, but I want you to realize that people are thinking the same thing about you, and if you aren't presenting yourself in a confident and powerful way, you may be causing yourself to get overlooked all too often by people who shouldn't.

There are two major benefits that go hand in hand with the ability to understand body language. They are:

1. The ability to present yourself in a way that is powerful, confident, and outgoing

2. The ability to read another person and get an accurate feel for how they are feeling, what they are thinking, and how you want to react to the situation

Both of these benefits are crucial to how you function in society.

Do you want to get that dream job, or promoted in the job you already work?

Do you want to have the confidence to pursue that dream or chase that goal?

Do you want to be able to know what is going on inside another person's head, and how you can respond to that?

Of course. The ability to do any of these things would put most people on top of the world. The only drawback is that they don't know how to get there. They sit in their homes dreaming up all of these things, then they go out into the world, keep themselves small and out of the way, then go home and dream some more.

I want to help you break out of that dream and start living it. Starting with how you are sitting right now, and ending in giving you the gift of understanding body language, this is a journey that is going to change your life.

When you are fluent in the art of body language, you are going to have the world at your fingertips.

Sound nice?

Then let's get started.

Chapter 2 – The Silence of a Thousand Words

You may find this surprising to hear at first, but we make major and serious life decisions based on the judgements we derive from body language. I know this sounds extreme at the beginning, but listen to these examples:

I could quote a lot of names and studies right now, but I want to keep this personal at the beginning. I'll follow up with all of the studies later on, but from your own life, I can show you how you use your judgements on body language to shape your actions.

You've seen interviews take place at your job. You may even be in charge to conducting those interviews. You have probably noticed then that the people who are hired are the ones that make the proper social cues. They make eye contact, they shake your hand with a firm handshake. They don't fidget, look around the room, or stutter.

All in all, they appear confident and competent, so they get the job.

But that is just one example. Consider your love life. If you see a man or a woman that you are attracted to, and you hope to get the attention of, you will automatically do things to get that attention. Perhaps you do the clichés of laughing loudly or talking loudly. Perhaps you do things to show off.

If you see that they are interested, it only adds fuel to the fire, but if you see that they don't care, that they have a ring on their finger, or that they just don't have an interest in you, the act stops.

You base what you do, based on what the other person does.

This is a truth that branches out even further than our social lives

In courtrooms, people who are under fire for one reason or another can hope to get a better outcome based on if the judge and jury like them. This is subliminal and often subconscious, but if their facial expressions, their eye contact, and their body cues in general impress those around them, they are given a lesser sentence, or perhaps set free all together.

Politicians are also part of this realm. In a Princeton study, it was shown that what we perceive in the facial expression of a politician in just a single second has over 70% influence on how we vote.

Why?

Because we put a lot of trust into our own perception of things. Not how things really are, but what we think they are.

Have you ever met someone, and found you had a mutual acquaintance? Perhaps this mutual acquaintance is someone you don't know well, but your new friend knows quite well. They start telling you all kinds of things you never knew about your mutual acquaintance, and you come to realize this is because you haven't ever asked.

You see this person, perhaps daily, but you never actually talk to them. Maybe it was the look on their face, which made you consider them to be unfriendly without even speaking. Perhaps it was the way they held their arms at their side, or the way they sat at lunch. It may have even been a combination of any of these things, but you realize you formed opinions on this person without ever speaking to them.

We do it this to people we meet on the street, we do it to people we are putting into positions of power over us, and we do it to each other every single day.

Consider this example:

You see one of your coworkers at work, someone that you usually see bright and cheery, but today they aren't smiling. Today, they keep their eyes on their work, don't move around much, and just have an all-around attitude of trying to keep to themselves.

From this, you derive that they must be in a bad mood. You don't know why, you don't ask why, you may not even care why, but you stay away from them and go about your own day, simply because of what you assume them to be feeling.

A perfect example of this is the trend in society to label certain people as having a "resting angry face".

If you have ever spent any time on social media, you know what this is. You may even be a person that has one. Someone that looks like they are unfriendly because of how their face is shaped.

They go through life, and are treated as though they aren't a very nice person, because of how their face looks in its normal countenance. There's countless jokes and clips made out of this idea, but if you analyze the reason behind this joke, you will see that I'm right.

We all form opinions and judgements on people based on nothing more than the look they have on their face. We then take it so far as to treat them a certain way, vote for them, or form a general opinion about them, all based on this perception we have of them.

Now, I'm not saying that this is right or wrong, but what I am saying is that it's true. And you can use this truth to your advantage by giving off the impression that you are confident, capable, and easy to get along with. If you carry yourself like a leader, you are going to be treated like a leader.

Chapter 3 – Mind Over Matter or Matter Over Mind?

Confidence is an elusive subject in the world we live in. They say that you either have it or you don't, and it seems as though the ones who are saying that are the ones who have it, and the ones who aren't... well, they're the ones who don't.

If you have been paying any attention at all up to this point, it is almost certain you know that have confident body language is going to take you far in life. The singular theme that presents itself over and over in this subject is the hierarchy of those who are dominant over those who are not.

Obviously, you want to succeed in life. Success is one of the three top things all of us seek after, but too many of us leave our success to a game of chance.

So many people think if they make it in life, they just got lucky, or the ones that do make it in life happen to be luckier than the rest of us, but I am telling you now those are lies you are telling yourself, and society is telling you. The people who are successful are the people who go out there and follow their dreams. They don't sit around and hope their dreams come to them.

You can be one of these people. You can sit back and hope that life throws you what you want (it won't) or you can get out there and pursue it. Even if you don't think you can do it, or if you don't feel like you can ever have that level of confidence, trust me, you can, and you will.

What comes first, the chicken or the egg?

So many times in life, if we want something, we have to make up our minds to get it, then go after it. For instance, if you want to lose weight, or if you want to have those six pack abs, you have to first decide in your mind that you are going to work out and eat right to get them.

You don't suddenly see the abs appear on your body, then make up your mind you want to eat right and work out, you have to make the decision first. The same goes for your bank account, a new job, or anything else you choose to pursue.

The desire may be there first (whether that be something material or emotional) but you have to make up your mind to get it before you can make your body do what you need it to do to get there. And, as you well know if you have ever tried to change your body in any way, that it is far from easy.

You might have that end goal in mind, with the body you want and the clothes you want, but the in between days are rough. Getting up, going to the gym, skipping the sugary snacks and going for the veggies... far from the fun you thought it was going to be.

But then, something incredibly happens. You start to see change in your body. You start to see your skin tightening up, and you start to see the definition of muscles forming. You start to see different muscles showing that you didn't know you had.

All of your hard work is paying off, and you now have the body you wanted.

Matter followed mind in this sense.

Our minds change our bodies, but do our bodies change our minds?

This has been the way of things for centuries. It is well-known if you want something to change, you have to make that decision in your mind first, then you will see the changes start to take place in your life.

But that line of thinking leaves little hope for those who want to be more confident, and to present themselves in a way the world is going to treat like a leader.

You see, if you think you have to have a certain mindset before you can achieve anything, then you are setting yourself up for failure in this realm, simply because confidence, leadership, and power are things few people are born into. Most of us have to build up our own confidence, and embrace that kind of mindset over time.

Sure, it's true that the more you embrace it, the more you will act like it, and the easier it is going to become all around, but the question remains: What are you going to do to gain confidence, if confidence comes from the mind, and your mind isn't confident?

The answer is simple in both concept and practice: You change your way of thinking.

That's right, if you are in the mindset that you have to think a certain way before you can act on it, then you won't ever be confident, because your mind won't let you be. You're always going to shrink back within yourself.

Why?

Because you are going to act like you feel. If you feel timid, then you will show yourself to be timid to the world. They will then feed off of that, and treat you like a follower. This, in turn, is going to make you feel more like a follower than a leader, thus trapping you in a vicious cycle.

Doesn't sound like a lot of fun, does it?

Thankfully, there is a different line of thinking that will free you from this cycle, and make it so you can develop the confidence you have been dreaming of. This, in turn, is going to show the world that you are a leader, and you will be treated like one.

I know the saying 'fake it until you make it' has been around for ages, but there is some truth to it.

The simple fact of the matter is that you can act a way you don't feel, and you can make those actions a habit, which will project to the world the kind of you that you want to show them. In other words, you can act like a confident leader, without being a confident leader.

Remember that you are the only person on the planet that knows what's going on inside your own head. You walk into a room, and you are the only person who knows what you are thinking, what your opinions are, what you think of the other people in the room, and so on.

This is a powerful tool when it comes to the act of projecting confidence. If you were to act confident when you walk into a room, no one is going to doubt that you are, in fact, they are going to form in their minds the opinion that you are a confident person before you even open your mouth.

Okay, that sounds easy enough, but how do I project being powerful and confident when I don't feel it on the inside?

That is a valid question. It is a challenge to look someone in the eye when you are terrified to do so, but that's when the mind comes back into play. If you make up your mind that you are going to act like a powerful person, then you can make yourself do it, even if you don't feel as though you are one.

To do this properly, you need to know how powerful people act, and learn how you can mimic it in your own life.

Powerful people tend to be more assertive, and act with greater confidence than those who are not

This statement is kind of obvious, as we have been talking about how you can gain greater confidence. But it's true, power and confidence go hand in hand. I think before we get into the confidence factor, we should take a second to look into the assertive factor first.

Assertion is acting out of the belief that you will be followed. In other words, you are saying how it is going to be, and you know that everyone is going to go along with it. There is a lot of things that go into this line of thinking, but at the forefront of it is the belief that you have good ideas, and they deserve to be followed.

If you want to be a more assertive person, the first thing you need to do is stop second guessing yourself. Sure, you might be second guessed, undermined, argued with, questioned, and so on, but you have to realize those are all external sources. If you want to have confidence in your ideas, then *you have to have confidence in your ideas.*

Go with your gut instinct. If you know how to do something, you think it will work done a certain way, or if you can imagine a better result, go with how you feel. Don't wait it out and seek the opinions of those around you, if they had good ideas, they would have given them. Their chance is gone now, and it's your turn.

If you start to assert yourself in this way, you are going to find that you have a following almost immediately. This is because all too many people are followers, and they are happy to do what any person with a sense of authority says.

I'm not trying to take away from your accomplishment in saying that, but rather, I am trying to show you that you have nothing to fear. One of the main reasons people hold back and don't voice their opinion is because they are afraid someone is going to argue with them or say they are wrong.

What I am saying is that first of all, if they do argue, who cares? Secondly, the odds are you won't even be argued with, because when you have the confidence to make a decision out loud, more often than not the people around you are going to follow it.

Powerful people are more confident in life in general.

Again, a pretty obvious statement, but we have to get into the confidence aspect at some point. Take a moment and think about a powerful person. It doesn't have to be anyone in particular, just someone. It can be someone you know personally, someone you've seen on tv, or someone you've read about.

Think about how they act in life. How they move, how they respond to the people around them, and how they go through their day. They make a decision, and they stick with it. They don't ask if that's all right with those around them, they don't seek out the approval of anyone else, they just go about their day, happy with the decision they make, and confident that it's going to work out.

They feel they are going to win whatever they participate in, even when it comes to games of chance.

What makes this interesting is they are even confident in realms that they have no control over. You will notice that it's the powerful people that make bold moves in gambles, it's the powerful people who put a lot on the line in deals they make, and it's the powerful people that will fund the most in an investment.

Now, I'm not talking about celebrities or tycoons here, I am talking about the people who live life powerfully. This can be anyone from the wealthiest man in the world to the guy who works part time at the gas station a block away from your house.

Powerful people tend to think about things more abstractly.

In order to fully understand what this means, it is important to understand the difference between concrete and abstract thinking.

Growing up, we are taught to use our imaginations. And to an extent, that is just what abstract thinking is. I don't mean you are thinking about talking purple dinosaurs per se, but you are able to think about things in general.

To simplify, instead of thinking of a particular dog... *your* dog, for example, think of dogs in general. Instead of thinking of that cat sitting on that window sill, think of the concept of space and how one thing can sit upon another.

Concrete thinking is what they nail into your brain when you reach adulthood, and in many ways, it is very important. If you can' think about something in a concrete manner, you are going to end up in the nut house. But, at the same time, never lose your ability to think about something in an abstract manner, either.

The more you keep this channel of your brain open, the easier it is going to be to keep it open in the long run.

They take more risks.

This point ties in closely to the point that they assume they are going to come out on top. If you have the mindset that it's going to work out for you, then you are going to also have the mindset that you can take more risks because, well, it's going to work out.

Powerful people do this in two ways... not only are they willing to take bigger risks, put more on the line, and gamble more with their decision, but they aren't going to let the outcome change what they do the next time.

What I mean by this is they are going to make the same gamble again in a different way later on. They aren't going to assume because this one didn't work out then the next one isn't going to work out, either. They just roll with the fact that you may win some, and you may lose some, but either way you know it's going to work out for you.

When you are developing your own sense of power and dominance, you need to let bumps in the road just be bumps in the road. A speed-bump that doesn't do anything to you in the long run, just a little glitch you have to run over right now.

Break out of that all or nothing kind of thinking. They say that you need to be all in or not in at all, but I disagree. Sure, there are things you need to devote yourself to, but in general, if something doesn't work out this time, it doesn't mean it isn't going to work out next time.

Pick yourself up, dust yourself off, and move on.

So what is this all coming down to?

I think you're going to like the answer.

We really can change how our mind thinks if we can change the action we are doing

Let's go back to that 'fake it until you make it' statement. There's a great truth here as well as something that isn't so true, and I think it's important to point out both.

The first thing I want to point out is that you can act a certain way, even if you don't feel it. You can present yourself as bold, confident, daring, powerful... anything you like even if you are melting on the inside. This is a good thing for all of you who want to embrace a more confident outlook.

What I do want to point out, however, as not true is the part of the saying that says you need to be fake until you make it. I feel this implies that you are going to be fake the entire time, and I know that some, if not all of you are going to have a problem with that.

No one wants to be fake. We all know that we can't live life as a fake, and that if we do try to live life this way, it is only a matter of time before we crack under the pressure and everything goes down the drain. I think a better way to look at this is to fake it until you actually do become it.

In fact, we could take the saying a step further (or change it all together) and say instead 'practice it until you become it'. Because you aren't ever being fake, you are growing and changing. You are in process of becoming through the practice you are doing.

In the chapters to come, we are going to look at the practical ways you can apply this to your life, and how you can actually put power into practice, and from there gain the confidence you have been looking for. Once you have that confidence, you are going to have the actions come naturally.

Right now, you may be doing things subconsciously, trying to make yourself appear more powerful already, and that's good! But I want you to consider one more thing before we close out this chapter:

Our nonverbal do govern how we feel

We tend to present ourselves in the way we feel about ourselves. If we go back to the analogy of the animal kingdom, none of those animals are doing anything different than how they feel. They puff themselves up because they really do feel like they are the best.

On the flip side of this, you need to take a look into your own life, and see how you are presenting yourself. If you are slumped down and taking up a minimal amount of space, ask yourself why. Ask yourself why you feel you need to sit that way, and why you hold yourself that way.

The practice is going to be the same regardless, but it is something you want to identify and keep in mind.

I get it, I have to make these changes in order to become a powerful and confident person, but if there are things I can do to make myself appear that way until I actually feel that way... what are they?

That's a very good question. We can all get caught up in the theoretical ideas of anything, but unless we have actual concrete things we can do then they end up just being ideas.

I have solid practical things you can do starting today that will put you directly on the path to being a more confident person, not to mention cause you to have some incredible and positive life changes from the beginning.

Starting in the next few chapters, we are going to look at the practical side of this practice, as well as the science behind all of it, and put you on the path to power.

Chapter 4 – The Method Behind the Madness

Remember when I told you in the earlier chapters that I was going to tell you the studies that back what I have been saying? Now's a good time to do that. There is actually a lot of science that goes along with this idea of self-presentation and our analyzing each other.

We already know at this point the qualities of powerful people, we know that we can change our actions to breed into ourselves the qualities that these powerful people have, and we also know that we can fake something (or practice something) until we become it.

There are certain thing that you can't just change about yourself, however, and they are things that you can't really ignore, either. Sure, you can work around them... virtually everything in life can be worked with or around in some way, but they are still things that you need to be aware of. Not to mention the science behind anything is simply fascinating, and it backs up the why behind it all.

First of all, let's take a moment to discuss hormones. The science of body language is more evident in the outside appearance of any individual, but let me assure you, there's definitely more to it than meets the eye. There are certain hormones that are very much involved in how we react to things, and something as simple as the balance of hormones in one person's body can make them vastly different than another person.

There are two main hormones that are involved in this area of study. They are Testosterone and Cortisol.

The reason these are the two hormones of interest is because they are the two hormones that relate to leadership. A person that is an ideal leader has the perfect balance between these two hormones, and that isn't a 50/50 split, either.

To better understand what I mean, let's take a look at each one separately, and put together what we find.

Testosterone is the dominance hormone

Most of us in life are familiar with Testosterone, at least to some extent. We all know that it is primarily a male hormone, but that women do have a level of it, too. We know that the more Testosterone a person has in their bloodstream, the more outspoken and aggressive they tend to be.

There is a reason for this, and that is because Testosterone is the dominance hormone. It is the hormone that is responsible for ruling over others, for elevating the confidence of the individual that has it, and for managing power.

It's a hormone that you can take supplements to get more of, but I recommend you hold off on that. The supplements are easily too much for your system, and you may end up with more problems than you want.

Cortisol is the stress hormone

The other hormone that is involved in this study is Cortisol. Now, Cortisol is the stress hormone. It is produced in both men and women equally, and it is produced when we feel stress.

You can take other things to suppress this hormone in yourself, anti-depressants being one of those things, but again I urge you to wait before you head for external interventions, as there are all kinds of ways you can manage these hormones without any outward help at all.

The reason I bring up these two hormones in particular is because they are the two hormones that show up in the testing of weak and powerful individuals.

There have been a number of tests done to try to determine the relationship between these two hormones in our bodies, and what we can do to balance them better.

The American Psychology Association ran a test on the two to determine how the mix of these hormones affects our social interactions. They say that the results varied, but in a study that was done by Princeton University, they found very consistent results.

Testosterone and Cortisol testing

In this test, 50 adults were taken into a room and had their baseline hormone levels taken. The results were recorded.

Then, they were directed to use power poses for 2 minutes. I am going to explain later on what power poses are and how you can also use them in your practice, but for now, focus on the hormones.

There are power poses that increase the feeling of power in our lives, and there are poses that decrease that feeling. The adults were simply told how to hold themselves for the two minutes, and weren't shown which poses were linked to power or weakness.

They were also tested in seclusion, there wasn't anyone else in the room during these two minutes, and after the two minutes, they were again tested for their hormone levels.

The results were astounding.

They found that all of the adults that were using the powerful power poses had an increase in Testosterone and a decrease in Cortisol. Both levels had changed dramatically.

But here's where it also gets interesting. They found that in all of the adults that were in the weakened power poses, hormones had taken the opposite turn. Cortisol was higher in these people than it was before, and Testosterone had dropped.

This, of course, led doctors to a whole new realm of questions.

If these adults responded to these poses after two minutes, is there a way that we can prepare ourselves for things that we need power for?

All they used was their own bodies and time... that is exactly what anyone has.

So, they conducted another experiment.

The Job Interview Experiment

It took a while for the doctors to decide what test they ought to do next. They wanted to have some sort of scenario that most anyone could relate to, and they finally decided that job interviewing was the way to go.

Most all of us have gone through that dreaded process, and most all of us dread having to do it again. With this in mind, they decided that this was the best choice of scenario as it is the most relatable.

So again, they selected a number of adults to take part in the study, and they chose a single person to conduct the mock interviews. The person that was conducting the interviews was to remain expressionless the entire time. Studies also show that we as people can't stand to talk to someone with no expression. We would rather be ridiculed, made fun of, yelled at, or pretty much anything besides dealing with lack of expression.

So again this new set of adults was instructed to go into these power poses for two minutes. They were to do this in the other room, alone, and wait for their turn in the interview. People out of sight watched and analyzed how the interview went from behind glass.

Again, the results were consistent and astounding. The people that engaged in the powerful power poses from the beginning were the ones that were confident in the room. They were open, outspoken, relaxed, and clearly more at ease than the people that were in the weaker power poses.

Upon further examination, these doctors realized that when most of us are waiting for a job interview, we are in the weakest pose while waiting. This does nothing for our confidence level except to damage it, and if we want to see better results in the interview room. We have to break this cycle.

But what do I mean we tend to be in the weakest power pose?

I am going to get into the actual list of poses in a little while, but I want you to think back in the earlier chapters when I pointed out how confident people take up a lot of space, and timid people take up minimal space.

When you are waiting for a job interview, what do you do? We tend to sit with our arms crossed. We look down at our phones or our notes, we cross our legs. Those are all things we subconsciously do when we feel insecure... which, as we learned already, if we do things that make us feel a certain way, it's only a matter of time before we start to really feel that way.

With that in mind, you can see how sitting this way before your job interview is going to negatively affect how it goes.

But, there's good news! If you want it to go better, you can see by these examples here proven facts that you can do things that will increase your confidence.

Ok, I can see how this all works together, but you said earlier that powerful people have a good balance of Testosterone and Cortisol. What exactly is that balance then?

A lot of people think that the more Testosterone they have, the better off they will be. They think they will be powerful, confident, tough, and able to move anything and everything out of their way. The problem with hormone supplements, however, is that it only raises one hormone, but doesn't do anything to the others.

You see, if you are a person that is highly stressed out, and you think you want to be more confident, the worst thing you can do is add Testosterone into your life. You are then going to feel rough and tough, but also incredibly stressed out.

Your stress is going to go up even further as you feel this way, because you will stress about why it isn't working. You will be more defensive, you won't feel any of the positives out of this experience, which, in turn, won't give you that confidence you need.

Power is also how you react to stress

.

It's a mistake to think that power is all glory. You are going to have your fair share of stress in life, no matter who you are or what position you hold. In fact, it seems that the more powerful a person is in life, the more stressful situations arise.

The key to effective power is to react to stress well. You can't ever eliminate it from your life, but you can learn how to respond to it in a healthy and non-invasive way. If you do this, you will feel your Testosterone levels increase, but at the same time your Cortisol levels are going to decrease. The combination of this is the exact match you are hoping for.

When you balance these two levels in this way, you will actually begin to feel powerful, and your confidence is going to rise.

Your increased confidence is then going to cause you to hold yourself in a powerful way, telling the world you are a confident person, just through your body language.

Tying it all together

There's a lot of information here that is very important to understand, but to summarize it now, you can see that:

You can manage your hormone levels by doing certain poses for a few minutes in a day. The better you are able to manage your hormone levels, the more confident you are going to feel.

The more confident you feel, the more your body is going to carry itself with confidence, which is going to balance out your hormone levels.

As you can see here, this is going to start in you a cycle, and that cycle is going to keep you in the powerful and confident mindset you are looking for.

So with this understanding in mind, let's move on to how you can effectively put this into practice, and start to build up that confidence in yourself.

Chapter 5 – Power Poses

Up until now, I have been talking a lot about the benefits of power poses. You were able to see how they can make incredible physical changes in a short amount of time, and you may be relieved to hear that you can do them anywhere and anytime.

Whether you need that little boost for a test, an interview, a date, or even just to walk into work or class like a boss, you can use power poses to make that happen.

Now, before I get into the different poses, I want you to understand the difference between the two groups of poses, and why they make a difference to you in your day. I am including a group of the low power poses, simply because I want you to avoid doing these.

You would be surprised how much you do these poses in your day, and how harmful they are to your overall outlook on the day. If you can make a double habit for yourself... the habit of practicing the empowering poses and the habit of avoiding the other poses, you are going to see and feel a dramatic increase in your body language almost immediately.

When you feel good, it shows in every part of your being.

Hi power and low power poses

I have referenced the two kinds of power poses several times now, but let's take an actual look at them, and what is going on for each pose.

High power posed people

We all see them, the people that walk into the room with their heads held high. They make eye contact, they aren't afraid to move their arms around. They don't try to make physical contact with the world around them, but you can tell they certainly aren't bothered by it if they do.

When they sit, they sit openly. They may cross their legs, but they cross it in such a way that you don't feel they are closed off. You can see they feel that they are worth something, and they have power in the room.

As a result, they are respected, and treated as though they have power. There isn't any hesitation to talk to them (unless the other person is feeling intimidated), they are actively sought out for advice and interaction, and they are treated as though they are people with power.

You notice that all of this has taken place when they never say a thing. There's no talk to make people think this about them, they just assume a lot of power and confidence based on the way the person is presenting himself.

Low power posed people

We all know that person with low power presentation. You may even be one of these people without even realizing it. To describe them, they are the person that sort of slinks into the room.

They avoid looking around, or making eye contact with anyone. They simply creep in, and creep to their spot, then sit with their arms drawn in at their side. They may cross their legs, but they don't do it in a way that is open, it is more of a way to minimize their presence in the room.

If they do need to draw attention to themselves, all they do is make a minimal show of it, they may raise their hand, they may actually speak, but they aren't going to do any of it in a way that draws any more attention to them than what is absolutely necessary.

These are people that we would describe as 'shy' or 'timid' or 'quiet', and while there's nothing wrong with being any of those things, these are also the people that are going to be looked over. They are going to be picked over when someone is after a person who is going to make change, and they may be the last person in the room anyone chooses for a partner for themselves.

Now, before you go and form any sort of judgement against these people, I want to make one thing clear. There isn't anything better about the power people than these people. The power people aren't smarter. They aren't more attractive, they don't have more money.

They aren't even more qualified to lead. The only difference about them and the people that are timid is how they present themselves. Sure, you can add in how they feel about themselves as well, but my point still stands. If you want to be a high power person, but you don't feel it, then just act like it.

You are just as qualified as anyone else, the only problem is how you are presenting yourself to the rest of the world. If you shake free of that and embrace opening up your power, then you are going to be the person that the rest of the world sees as powerful.

How to do the high power poses

So now, the big reveal. How do you become that person? What are these exercises that you need to do that are going to open up your confidence and give you that boost you need?

The high power poses. These are the only things you need to do. You need to do them for 2 minutes before you engage in a stressful activity of any kind. Whether you are going on a date, in for a test, in for an interview... anything that you could use that bit of a boost for, do these.

It literally takes 2 minutes, that's 120 seconds out of your day, and the outcome of your day is going to go infinitely better.

The star pose

Very self-explanatory, you stand with your feet outspread, and your arms out in a V position, almost as though you were celebrating a goal. Hold this for a couple of minutes. Breathe in and breathe out.

You can do this in front of a mirror if you have it, and see how you look. Open, in control, able to handle anything that comes your way. When you are able to do this for a full 2 minutes right before you go into a stressful situation, you will find that the situation goes so much better. It is as though you are suddenly capable of anything you like.

The wonder woman pose

You stand with your feet in the same position, but instead of having your arms outstretched, you put them on your hips. I know you've seen Wonder Woman do this, but if by some chance you have not, then look her up on the internet and you will see exactly what I mean.

It is a very easy pose to hold, and one that is very rewarding for the comfort that you feel when you do it. You could even tell yourself that you are your own hero and you are going to go into this with power.

By the time you are finished with your two minutes, you are going to feel like you really can take on any villain that is headed your way, and whatever you are preparing for is going to seem like nothing at all.

Another benefit of this pose is that it takes less room to do than the other one, so if you want to keep private while you do this, you are going to have an easier time keeping in a small space while you prepare.

The sitting down star

You can also do power poses while you sit down. Sometimes, you aren't going to have the opportunity to stand in preparation for whatever you are going through. You might be in a bus, you might be in a cab. You might be on a plane or in a waiting room or a classroom.

No matter where you have to sit, however, you are going to still be able to do your poses. All you have to do with this pose is sit with your arms bent at the elbows, and your hands behind your head.

Sit back in the chair, recline as though you don't care what is going on around you. Act as though you own the place, and look as though you know you do. You can also add more to this look by bringing up your ankle and placing your ankle on your knee.

Don't cross your legs at the ankles or put your knee on the other one, if you want to do this the right way, you need to keep as open as possible as you work at it, and keep the attitude that you are there to win, and you know you are going to.

The leaner

There are times when you can stand, but you don't have all the room to do the standing star pose or the wonder woman pose. Or perhaps you are in the middle of a room and you don't want to draw that attention to yourself.

First of all, this is just fine. You are doing these exercises to make yourself feel powerful. To do this, you may want to have privacy, and that may be just what you need to succeed.

But, if you aren't going to get that privacy, then the best way to go about it is to do the leaner pose. This is a very easy and subtle pose you can do. You can do it in front of a room of people and they won't have any idea that's what you're doing, and you can look entirely natural doing it.

To do this pose, you need a chair, a counter, or a table. All you do is stand next to it, and place both of the palms of your hands on top of it. Lean forward but stand up as tall as you can. Stand as though you are speaking with someone on the other end of the table, and you are leaning in to make your point.

Stand as though you aren't going to back down, and you know you are going to win your point if you hold your ground. Stand up and stand tall, drawing yourself up from the floor with deliberation.

If you stand like this for the two minutes, you are going to get the same effect as you would if you were to do any of the other poses, but you can do this in front of a room of people and no one is going to think twice about what you are doing. You may look like you are leaning toward the bathroom mirror, trying to get a better look at yourself.

If you are next to a table or a chair, you are going to look like you are lost in thought. No matter how or where you do this, people are going to assume you are in charge of something, and you are taking a moment to analyze it. No one is going to think you are nervous or scared and are taking a moment to get it all back together.

As I have said before, you don't need to have that perfect feeling right now, you don't need to be where you want to be right now. All you have to do is look like you're there, and you will feel like you're there in no time.

Low power poses to avoid in everyday life

Now, as we saw in the previous chapters, there are things you do because you may feel a certain way about yourself. You may really be shy or timid, and the way you carry yourself only confirms that.

But, if you don't feel that way about yourself, you may be projecting that out there if you aren't careful, and if you are trying to land that date or get the attention of that supervisor, you aren't going to be doing yourself any favors.

If you want to keep your poise, then you need to learn how to keep your pose. As a habit of life, avoid doing these things, and own the room you walk into, from the moment you walk into it.

Never hold your hands together, especially if you are touching both of your elbows. You might do it out of habit, but you look like you are trying to draw yourself in.

Never touch your neck, this is the height of vulnerability. While we may not hunt or be hunted like we once did, we still see those cues given off by each other, and the opinions we form of those that do this isn't an opinion you want someone to form of you.

Never cross your legs to make yourself small. This is going to make you look uncertain, and like you don't know what you are doing with yourself. You need to be open, ready to take in the world as it comes. The best way to do this is to look like you could talk to anyone at any time.

You don't have to actually go around or strike up any conversations. The point of this isn't to speak. Remember, this is all what is said through your own body language. So let your body speak for itself. Let your attitude shine forth, and let the right opinions come in around you.

If you make an effort to practice this regularly, you are going to be able to keep your hormones in balance, keep your confidence up, and keep the world thinking just what you want them to think, all at the same time.

Presence is everything

In a nutshell, all of what I am saying here is that you want to have a good presence. If you were in the performing industry, they would call it stage presence. You want to own your own atmosphere.

You don't have to take this the wrong way. Don't go around being obnoxious or feeling like you have to be the life of the party, but don't go the other way with it, either. If you want to own the room, then you need to own your own room.

Have the presence about you that says you know who you are. You know you have a purpose and you intend to fulfill it. You are interesting, and you know it. You are capable, and you know it.

Basically, anything you want to be, you believe you are that, and you can add on the fact that you know it afterward. They say that you shouldn't ever be arrogant in what you do, but they also say that you need to have that confidence to shine out of the crowd.

When you are timid or when you always try to blend in to the area around you, one of two things happens. Either you do blend in, which means you aren't doing yourself any favors. Or you don't blend in, but rather you stand out as the person that is shy or scared.

Either one of these are things you want to avoid. You are worth the time and effort that anyone could give you, so look like you expect it. The more you believe in you, the more the rest of the world is going to, too.

Tiny tweaks can lead to big changes in your life

I hate to be the one to point it out, but in the grand scheme of things, these are very minor changes to what you are doing in your day. All I am really asking you to do is keep your head up, keep your chest up, and act like you mean it.

Stop slinking around, and make that eye contact. Tell the world with your body that you know you are powerful, and you know you can handle anything that is coming your way.

My point in saying this is that you don't have to make a 180 in your life. You don't need to pull out your notepad and jot down all of these changes you need to do in order to be successful, all you have to do is change a few areas in how you sit and stand.

Little things you do in your day can lead to massive changes over time. All you have to do is stay consistent and you will feel the change take place inside of you.

So stick with the small. Don't go off track with big delusions that you have to be bigger or better. You do deserve your dream, and you deserve what you want to be in life. What I am challenging you to do is to make those little changes that are going to get you to where you need to be.

Try a power pose and share the love

Now that you know the secret to gaining instant confidence, I want you to put it into practice. You need to go into the bathroom, right now, no matter where you are or what you are doing.

This is literally only going to take two minutes of your time, so don't act like you don't have the two minutes to spare to make a change in your life. Pick out one of the poses, and head into a place where you can have two minutes to yourself.

Time yourself and do the pose for two minutes, and see the change take place immediately. I know there's going to be a major difference in how you feel both before and after, but there is also going to be a difference in how you feel between doing it for fun and doing it to get ready for something big.

Once you are comfortable in the pose, use it the next time you need that boost for real, and see how you feel. See how the interaction goes, and see how you feel about it afterwards as well.

When you see this all come together as you want it to, it's time to spread the love. This is a method that works, and we want to get the help out to as many people as possible, so let your confidence shine, and let the world grow right along with you!

Chapter 6 – The Secret Handshake

In the world we live in, one would think that it's what you wear, what you drive, and where you work that causes people to form opinions about you. Surprisingly, this isn't at all the case.

Experts say that it takes four minutes to form your basic opinion about a person. Four minutes. In that time, unless they are just trying to show off to you, you won't know anything about where they live, what they drive, or perhaps even what they do for a living.

The things you are going to base this opinion on are things you may not even realize. Minor physical things.

Eye contact, how they are standing, and how they shake your hand.

That's right, how a person shakes your hand... or how you shake another person's hand... is one of the key points in forming opinions about each other.

With this in mind, let's take a look at hand shaking, and find out what your handshake says about you.

Where did the handshake come from?

If you spend any time thinking about it, shaking hands is a rather odd thing we do in our society. When you meet someone for the first time, when you seal the deal on a business interaction, or when you are parting ways in a formal gathering, you shake hands.

Perhaps the most nerve wracking handshake is the one you give when you are meeting someone for the first time.

The tradition springs out of ancient Rome. On the battlefield, after a victory was won the generals would greet each other with a clasping of the hands. They would to this slightly different than we do today, in that they would stand closer together and raise their arms up higher.

Part of the reason they would do this is to determine who got the first cut of the spoils. Whichever general had his hand on top, even if it was only slightly, would get to have the first run of the wine and bounty.

This is where our term "having the upper hand" comes from.

What your handshake says about you

If the two generals were to clasp hands, and the grip was the same for both of them, they would split their spoil and celebrations right down the middle, and begin at the same time. With this being the case, each general would try to match the other's grip.

With that in mind, let's bring it back to the here and now. Do you give a good handshake? What is your handshake telling the world?

For starters, we all tend to do handshakes improperly. Men come on too strong and forceful as a habit of life, and women tend to offer a limp hand. It usually is habit, but it's something you can work around no matter what you do.

The reason I am concerned about you giving a good handshake is because that serves to help the people you meet form an opinion about you.

A too strong handshake

You may have heard when you meet someone, you need to offer them a nice, firm hand. This is true to an extent. You do need to give them a firm grasp, but you don't need to overdo it.

A handshake that is too strong is going to come off as domineering, and may intimidate the person you just met. While you may think this is a good thing at first, consider the fact you don't want to intimidate your potential employer, or someone you are trying to ask out on a date.

Aim for strong, but not too strong.

The limp noodle

As I said, women tend to offer a weak handshake more than men, and this is largely unintentional. They do so because they are either nervous, intimidated by the situation, or trying to appear feminine.

There's nothing wrong with being feminine, but you can't let that come forth in your handshake. The reason for this is because we subconsciously determine who has the 'upper hand' when we meet someone for the first time, and if you are offering a hand that is just limp, the person you are meeting is going to determine that you will do just about anything they want.

Now, that's not to say they are going to think that or ask it right out, but that's the general impression they get, and that's what I want you to be aware of. You want to show them you are feminine, but that you can hold your own in the situation.

Just right

A perfect handshake, or the handshake that is 'just right', is a handshake that is equal on both sides. Equal pressure is administered, equal force in the handshake, and it is executed for equal amounts of time.

Nobody has the upper hand, because both are the same. You meet in the middle, you show each other you have the same force behind your shake, and you let it go at the same time.

It's a very simple idea in concept, and beautiful when executed, but you have to practice.

How to effect the perfect handshake

When people try to execute the perfect handshake from the beginning, they tend to be too strong. Women especially will overcompensate for their action, and end up squeezing too hard and pumping their hand like their running an old fashioned mining cart.

Men tend to go the other way with it, and if they try to ease up their force, they hardly apply any pressure, giving off the impression they aren't confident.

But, there's hope. You really can accomplish the perfect handshake, it just takes a little bit of practice to get it done.

Step 1.

The first thing you do when you are going in for a handshake is to offer your hand perfectly straight. Hold your hand in front of you, with your thumb upward, and your pinky on the bottom.

You will notice when you do this that your hand naturally tilts one way or the other. It may not be by much, and you really have to look to see which way yours tips, but I promise you that it does.

Now, practice straightening it out, and extending it in this straight fashion. Again, this is going to take a bit of practice as you may over compensate in one way or the other. Your goal is to reach straight out with your hand perfectly upright.

Once you have this down, you're ready to move on to step two.

Step 2.

Once your hand meets the other person's hand, you immediately gauge the pressure they are applying, and you aim to match it. If a handshake is done perfectly, both people have their hands clasped upright, palms together, and the same amount of pressure is applied on both sides.

Both people will feel good about this interaction, and neither is going to come away intimidated or feeling dominant.

Step 3.

Going back to when your hands meet, you apply equal pressure on both sides, and you look each other in the eye. You will notice that something happens as you do this.

If you both look each other in the eye and apply the same amount of pressure, the handshake is going to feel natural, you will pump at the same time, for the same amount of time.

If something isn't right, however, the handshake is going to also end up off. If he person you are meeting refuses to look you in the eye, or only looks for a second then looks away, they are going to immediately give off the impression they aren't sure of themselves, and you will naturally grasp their hand a bit harder. You have to work to control this, and practice to keep the same pressure on the hand no matter what they do.

Again, if the handshake is well matched, you will both engage for the same amount of time naturally, but if the other person looks away, they may not initiate any of the handshake, and you are left to take care of the entire thing yourself.

Don't stand there and shake and shake their hand. Just a couple of up down motions is plenty, then release and move on with the interaction. While you may have a firm grasp to your handshake, you will still give the impression of nerves if you pump for too long.

Do people really analyze hands that much?

Consciously, no, not everyone puts that amount of time and energy into shaking hands, but subconsciously, we can't help it. Just as we are always analyzing the behavior of the world around us, we also analyze the fine details without ever realizing we are.

You gauge your actions based on your own analysis, and others base their actions on the same front, only when others do it, they are analyzing you.

Chapter 7 – The Power of the Palm of Your Hand

So many times in advertisements you see the power of something that fits in the palm of your hand. The analogy here is clearly because the palms of your hands aren't very big, and to think you can get such power to fit inside them is a wonder you would like to have.

But, we must not be so quick to belittle the palms. These are very intricate and valuable parts of our body. The brain has more connection to the palm of your hand than it does to any other part of your body.

This may sound incredible at first, but when you realize all of the things you can do with your hands, from working on the most elaborate building to adding the smallest details on the tiniest piece of artwork, you get a bigger feel for what I am talking about.

But, there is more to the hands than meets the eye.

Without even realizing it, we use our hands in communication every single day. We use them to give instructions, we use them to explain things, we use them to ask, and we use them to direct.

It has been tested and proven that you can get what you want by simply making the right motion with your hands as you are speaking.

Example:

A speaker stood in front of an audience full of people. He said the same thing to the audience three different times, using the same posture, the same body language, and the same tone of voice all three times. Nothing about him changed at all, except for what he did with the palms of his hands as he spoke.

His goal was to make the audience do as he asked, and follow the directions he gave them as he spoke. The 3 audiences were not connected in any way, and they were randomly selected people. They had no idea what was going on or what they were supposed to do, just that they were to either do as the speaker asked, or not, based on what they felt they wanted to do.

The first time the speaker spoke to them, he kept is palms up. He made wide, sweeping gestures as he asked them to change seats all over the room.

The second time he spoke, he used his fingers to point, but he used all 4 of his fingers, to point out where he wanted them to sit and what they could choose to do.

With the last audience, he used only a single finger as he spoke. He pointed with his index finger from one side of the room to the other, but he kept the same tone of voice, stood in the same manner, and made the same amount of eye contact as he did each time.

The only thing that was different about his actions was what he did with the palms of his hands as he spoke.

At the end of the 3 sessions, the audiences were all interviewed. They were asked to recall how much of what was said, how much of the directive they remembered, how they would describe the speaker, and how they felt about the situation as a whole.

They were also asked if they would follow the directions the speaker gave them or not, based on the simple fact of how he asked them.

The results of the interviews were incredible. The audience that saw the speaker use his palms up position retained 40% more of what he said then the audience who viewed him with his palms down. The first audience would describe him as fun, laid back, easy to get along with, and so on, while the audience that saw him with his palms down described him as managing, pushy, and so on.

As soon as you got to the audience that saw him use a single finger in his directive, they found that the people didn't recall much at all about what was said, and they had very harsh words to describe the speaker.

Remember that the speaker had the same tone of voice and body language through all of this. He only changed what he did with the palms of his hands as he spoke, and the results were that varied.

So the challenge for you is to analyze what your primary position is with your hands as you speak to people.

Most people don't ever think about this. You may interact with people how you think you should, but you may not ever realize what you are doing with your hands, or how they can be damaging to what you want others to do.

Think about it, you have a lot more dominance in your tone when you put your hands facing palm down. To put a finer point on it, your hand is 4 times more powerful when it is face down rather when it is face up. The gesture is scarier, the look is fiercer, and the all-around tone to the body is one of dominance.

After all, what would the Nazis have looked like when they saluted Hitler if they had put their palms up? If you can imagine it for a second, you can see that they would go from a scary pose to one that is almost comical.

If you have a hard time thinking of what you do yourself as you interact with people, just take a few days and keep track of what you are doing. For this time, don't change how you act, just watch yourself interact with others, and see what you are doing with your hands as you do so.

You can even take this a bit further and note what you do with your tone and overall body language as you interact with people, because it is entirely natural for us to change our tone of voice along with our body language.

You can practice and change what you do with your hands as you are interacting with people. It takes a bit of time and effort, but it won't be long

before you are able to control what you are doing based on the situation.

The one thing you have to remember is that your body language is a reflection of how we feel on the inside. We saw this in the earlier chapters of this book, and you have probably noticed it around the people you know.

You can see this when you look around the room and can make an accurate guess on how people are feeling based on how they look. It is a known fact that you look how you feel, but we need to take a moment to dive into this further, and actually change how you feel based on your actions.

I know we have already looked at practicing until you become it, but did you know you can influence the world around you by this same attitude? In the past sections, we looked at how you can look like you are powerful, when you may not be, but you can get that position of leadership because of how people view you.

Now, I want to show you the palm method of convincing people. Do this when you want to influence people to get that yes. This whole book has been about using body language to your advantage, but there is only so much you can do when you look confident.

In the next chapter, we are going to dive into how you can read people and see what is going on inside their heads, but for now, we are still going to take a few minutes to look at you and what you can do to get that influence.

Let's take what we learned from the audiences and the speaker to learn what you can do in your own personal situations.

The first speaker kept his hands up. He did this while he used the same directions and tone of voice, but he got the highest response. This is because when palms are facing up, you sound welcoming. You sound like you want to encourage the people to do what you say.

They feel like you are on their side. You're their friend, and it doesn't matter what you ask them to do, it's going to be a good idea. The other audiences didn't feel this way at all, in fact, they largely didn't want to do as the speaker asked because of the way he held his hands, even though his message and posture were the same.

So how can you use this in your day to day speech?

Practice. There are going to be times when you need to use your finger or palms facing down. If you are giving directions in the instance of an emergency, you can't put your palms up, because that gives off the impression you don't know what the best course of action is and everyone has to fend for themselves.

But, if you get in the habit of keeping your hands faced palms up in your normal speech, you are going to be that person everyone wants to listen to.

As we saw, it only takes about 4 minutes for a person to form an opinion about you, and whether that opinion is true or false doesn't really matter. Once they have that opinion, it is next to impossible to get them to change their mind.

This means if you have the habit of using your hands in a directive way, you are going to instill in them the negative kind of opinion you don't want them to have. Instead, you need to adopt the palms up method. This is going to give off the impression that you know what you are talking about, that you only care about what is best for them, and you want everyone to be happy.

Use sweeping gestures when you speak, and give the impression you are all about them. I know this sounds like manipulation when you read it at first, but again, I am going to remind you that you don't need to use manipulation to get what you want. Never say anything you don't mean. Never do anything you don't mean.

Only change the way you are interacting with the world around you, and see the changes take place. I can't emphasize enough how much we as people are influenced by the actions and posture of the people around us. We hear tones of voice, we see the situation at hand, but we react to the body language that the person has.

Pay attention to what you do as a habit of life, and practice what you can do to make it better.

Once you know what you do with your hands, you can then change it to match the open method. It is going to take time, especially if you are in the habit of being more directive. But, once you have your open palms in mind, it is going to become a lot easier to manage than you would initially think.

You can gauge how you are doing based on the response of the people around you, and adjust what you do according to what they are doing. If you need soften your gestures, do it subtly. Don't be wild, and don't toss your hands around.

We respond better to the subtle things. Without even realizing it, these are the movements that we look at first, and the ones that stick with us the longest. If you want to make the largest impression on a person, then make the smallest, softest, and most welcoming movements that you can.

Once you have mastered the ability to hold yourself with confidence, and the keys to interacting with people, you are ready to move on to the final section of body language.

Reading it.

In the next chapter, we are going to take a look at the world around you, and how people commonly react to different feelings. You can use this information to change and influence the people around you, and use that to your greatest benefit.

Chapter 8 – Reading Body Language

Up until this point, we have been studying how to improve your body language to tell the world you know who you are and what you are after. This is going to aid you greatly in anything you pursue in life, whether it be related to your career, your academics, your love life, or anything else you can imagine.

There's another side to body language, however, it's well worth your time to study. You may be a master at *speaking* your body language, but how versed are you in *reading* other people?

What is society silently telling you?

We've all been there, stuck in the middle of a busy intersection with cars blaring their horns at us, or unable to move out of the way when there are people in line behind us. Nobody has to tell you that they are angry, they do a fine job of showing it, even without saying anything at all.

Yes, there are times when the body language of those around us is blatantly obvious. No one has to tell us what they are feeling or thinking. But then, there are times when you feel like you are speaking to a stone wall, and you would give anything to see inside that person's thoughts.

Perhaps it's your first date and you hope it's going well, but she hasn't said too much. Maybe you are dying to get that new position at work, but your boss has been interviewing a lot of people, and you want to know how yours went.

There's the negotiations that take place on a daily basis, whether we are trying to purchase a new car, or get a good sale on the vehicle that's been in the garage for months now. Maybe you're trying to talk down the price on a bike for your kid.

Whatever the case behind it, you want to know how your conversation is going, and what the other person is thinking.

Think about it, if you knew what was going on inside the head of someone you were negotiating with, speaking with, trying to impress, etc.... could you do something to change the outcome of the situation?

As much as any of us hate to admit it, it's true. If you knew what was going on insider her head, you may have done something differently to get a better chance at a second date. If you knew how to react to your boss's questions, you might be able to give better answers to increase your chances of getting that job.

Some call this manipulation, but that is merely because they don't understand how it works. You aren't saying things to get your way, you are reacting to a situation that has arisen differently because you have a better understanding of what is going on.

The ability to read another person is going to give you that ability. If you follow the subtle things they do during the interaction, you can change what you are doing to make them happy, and give them what they want. This, in turn, is going to come back to you as you will then get what you want.

So, let's get started.

Reading people 101: the basics

There are a few things you should know right off the bat that will greatly change the way you interact with people. Here are a few of the basic things to keep an eye out for that will help you know what move you should make next.

Arms crossed, folded in, or touching the neck.

A person you see doing this is feeling shy, nervous, or closed off. Any of these emotions means that they don't want to be ambushed, so you need to approach slowly.

Lighten up the mood with simple conversation, and avoid topics that are sensitive or personal at this point. If you are prying too deeply right now, you could potentially cause them to close up even further. Instead, focus on the neutral, the happy, and the things that can get the conversation flowing.

Avoiding eye contact.

Again, another sign of nerves. A person that isn't making eye contact is someone that isn't sure of themselves. This could be for a number of reasons, but remember, it isn't your place to judge the cause of the feeling, just what they are feeling.

Tight smiles.

When a person smiles naturally, there are things that happen to their face that are completely out of control. A genuine smile is going to cause the eyes to wrinkle... if you have ever hear the term "crow's feet" this is what it is talking about.

Older people get this naturally as they age, but if someone is smiling a genuine smile, no matter how old they are, they are going to get this around their eyes.

You can gauge for yourself the situation, and if you see that the smile is genuine, you know how to proceed, but if you can see if it's a forced smile, you may want to reanalyze how you are going about things.

Reaching out or touching

If you are in conversation with someone, and they reach out and touch you, it is a sign they are comfortable and happy with the situation. This can be as subtle as putting a hand on your shoulder or your forearm, or as open as a straight up hug.

Another thing to watch for is when a person has their feet pointed toward you. Whenever we as people are interested in a person, whether it be romantically, socially, or for any other reason, we tend to face them. It is entirely subconscious, and very few people know to look for this, but if you have the attention of the person you are speaking to, you're going to see it in their body.

Stepping back or lifting hands up

This is a reaction to an uncomfortable situation. People will do this for a number of reasons, but the underlying issue is that they feel uncomfortable and that is the natural way to react.

Think of it as backing away from danger. While that is a rather extreme way of putting it, you can still get a feel for what the person is feeling on the inside, even if that's not what they think they feel.

If you see this happening, you may be coming off a bit too strong, and you need to ease up a bit.

Remember, one of the biggest keys to effective communication is to keep the mood light.

But what do these actions mean to me?

It can be hard to give solid examples of how you should use each of the actions, or any of the actions for that matter, but what I do want is for you to have an understanding of what is going on.

I'm sure you have been in situations that could have turned out differently if you had known how to respond to what was going on, but when you are in certain situations, it can be difficult. For example, when you are on that first date, both of you are nervous, and the other person may not want to offend you by saying what's on their mind.

If you can see what they are feeling based on how they are acting, however, you can alter the situation to make it better for you.

So many couples start out by saying it seemed as though they could read each other's mind, and if you can manage to give off that impression, you greatly increase your chances of getting another date.

In the business realm, or even in the academic realm, if you can see how the boss or teacher is feeling based on their body language, you know what you should do instead. You can add things into an interview that may help you get the job, or you can know to stop repeating the story you are telling because you see that it's not sitting well with your interviewer.

All of these things are subtle, even your reactions to the body language, so you have to practice to know both what is happening and how you should respond.

With practice, you are going to get a feel for what is going on, and learn how you should react to it. Remember, by now you have that open, powerful body language yourself, which many come off as intimidating to some people. All in all, you have to practice.

The more you work at it, the more comfortable you are going to be. You will learn how to wield yourself in a way that is open and friendly, but also commands attention. You will learn how to read the people around you, and base your actions off of what they are feeling, and you will learn how to speak the language.

I hope you take the time to learn this well. Your entire world is going to change right along with your ability to read this language. I know you have what it takes to make it, and that you can master the language in no time at all.

Good luck!

Conclusion

Thank you again for purchasing this book!

I hope this book was able to help you to learn the secrets behind body language, and how to read another person effectively.

The next step is to put what you have learned into practice. You can't get better at anything if you don't practice it, and that includes anything that deals with other people. If you want to truly master social interaction, you have to master the ability to read people, and that's not going to just happen.

As intricate as learning a new language, you have to study and apply what you learn. Put it into practice and work on it, and next time you are in a social setting, use what you have learned to interact with the people around you.

It may seem difficult at first, and you will always have people that are harder to read than others, but with a trained eye, you will be able to glean any information you want from any person you speak with.

Have fun and learn as you go along, and you will get the benefits you are after.

Finally, if you enjoyed this book, then I'd like to ask you for a favor, would you be kind enough to leave a review for this book on Amazon? It'd be greatly appreciated! If you did not like the book, could you please help me making it better? Send me a email using this address: harveysegler@gmail.com. Tell me what you think I should do different.

Go to amazon.com to leave a review.

Now to your FREE gift! I am working with a company which has an email list where you can great offers and info about books on $2.99, $0.99 or FREE promotions.

Do you want to join it? It is 100% free for you if you use the link below and they guarantee that there will be no spam whatsoever. 1-2 emails a week with some book tips, that's it.

(Obs. You have the paperback version. Go to amazon to download the online version of this book for free and get the special link)

Thank you and good luck!

Made in the USA
San Bernardino, CA
02 February 2018